Tomato

COLOPHON

Recipes: Thea Spierings
Editor: Klary Koopmans
Final editing: Elles van Genugten
Art design: Myrthe Bergboer
Design: Inge van den Elzen
Photography: Jurriaan Huting, Remco Lassche,
Food4eyes.com
Food stylist: Lize Boer
Assistant publisher: Josje Kets
Publisher: Pieter Harts

With thanks to:
Bongers Agencies, Kahla Porselein, Stippels,
David Mulder, Dill & Kamille, Vroom & Dreesmann

© Visconti
1st edition 2008

ISBN: 978-90-8724-088-2

© English edition: Miller Books
e-mail: info@miller-books.com
www.miller-books.com

Tomaat

pomodoro

tomate

Tomato

tamatie

tomat

tomate

pomàta

Foreword

There are certain foods which you just can never get enough of. They will always surprise and inspire you, and when you see them in the shops, you immediately get that feeling of wanting to get to work. These are the main players in **My favourite ingredient**: a series which is a tribute to our favourite ingredients. In each book, one ingredient is put under the spotlight. Splendid photographs and 40 easy to prepare recipes (from snacks to main dishes, with flavours from every continent) give you an abundance of inspiration to discover its diversity.

This book is about the **tomato**. Come join us on an adventure!

Sweet and sunny fruit

What would the world be without tomatoes? Almost everywhere you will find tomato dishes - from Italian pizza to Indian curry, from Spanish gazpacho to Mexican salsa. In particular, the Mediterranean cuisine uses abundantly these sunny, sweet fruit, which makes it all the harder to believe that there was once a time (not that many centuries ago) when nobody in Europe had ever heard of the tomato. From the two centimetres of a large cherry tomato to the ten centimetres of your average beef tomato: it's no longer possible to imagine cooking without tomatoes. And you can make so much more than just salad, tomato soup and spaghetti sauce. This little book with its 40 surprising tomato recipes is the proof.

History

Together with other now ubiquitous ingredients such as the potato, chocolate, chilli peppers, peppers and corn, the tomato only came to Europe and Asia after the colonisation of North and South America by the Spanish. At the beginning of the 16th century, the first tomato seeds were brought to Europe, the tomatoes which were cultivated were in fact yellow and not red. This explains the Italian name of the fruit, pomo d´oro, golden apple. The tomato became red after crossing and refining the various tomato strains. Our word tomato is derived, just like the naming of tomato in many other languages, from the Aztec word tomatl, which means something like plump fruit. The first European tomatoes were not eaten but created to be admired:

as decorative plants in the garden, and the fruit as a decoration on table. People were a little bit fearful of this new fruit. Not so surprising if you consider that the tomato does in fact belong to the deadly nightshade family, and indeed the stalks and leaves are not particularly good for you. Spain and Italy were the countries where the tomato became popular very quickly: the very first book with tomato recipes appeared in 1692 in Naples. Northern Europe followed shortly thereafter, and it would be another couple of hundred years before the tomato triumphed completely all over the world.

Tomato cultivation

In countries with a temperate climate, such as the Netherlands, tomatoes are cultivated in greenhouses. The season runs from March to November. But nowadays in some greenhouses, they are cultivated all year round with special grow lamps so that we can also enjoy ripe tomatoes during the winter. The time when there was only one type of tomato in the shops is fortunately long past. There are all sorts of varieties available, from the small cherry tomatoes to giant beef tomatoes, which all differ in sweetness and firmness. And there is even once again the

yellow tomato of yore! In general the following principle holds good: the smaller they are, the sweeter they are. Vine tomatoes ripen longer on the plant, which gives them more taste. Roma or plum tomatoes (elongated in shape) have a firmer flesh and are therefore perfect for salads.

Buying and storing

Tomatoes love the sun and warmth. For this reason, never keep tomatoes in the fridge: at temperatures below 13 degrees Celsius they suffer from low temperature decay, and become bland and tasteless. You can quite simply keep your tomatoes in the fruit

bowl at room temperature, where they will continue to ripen and become even nicer! A damaged tomato will rot quickly; so pay attention when you buy your tomatoes that there are no soft spots or damaged peel.

Vegetable or fruit?

Botanically, the tomato is considered to be a berry, and thus a fruit. However we consider it to be a vegetable, which means that we only use tomatoes in savoury dishes. Although we love our tomatoes, you won't readily

come across a tomato sorbet or tomato biscuits!

Store for later

For centuries, people have been trying to conserve the sun-matured tomato taste for the dark wintertime. Tinned tomatoes, tomato sauce, tomato ketchup, tomato purée and sun-dried tomatoes are all products which make it possible to cook with tomatoes during all seasons. The most well known are tinned tomatoes, whether they be chopped

The healthy tomato

Due to the pigment lycopene, the tomato is beautifully red. Lycopene works as an antioxidant, which apparently offers protection against cancer. To make optimal use of this, it is better to eat heated tomatoes, ketchup and tomato sauce, since there are greater concentrations of lycopene in them than in raw tomatoes.

Furthermore, there are vitamins A and C in tomatoes, they contain few carbohydrates, and they are low in fat and high in fibre. Thus, they fit in well with a health-conscious eating pattern.

Peeling tomatoes

More often than not, it is nicer (and more attractive) to remove the skin of the tomato before using them in a recipe. This is very easy: with a sharp knife make a cross on the bottom of the tomato. Put the tomato in a pan or a baking dish and pour boiling water on top. After a couple of seconds, you'll notice the skin lifting. Do not leave the tomatoes to stand too long in the hot water. Strain and then rinse them in cold water, it is then easy to remove the skin.

or not. With a flick of the wrist, a soup or sauce is prepared in an instant. Tomato purée is made from thickened tomato sauce: it no longer resembles real fresh tomatoes, but in small quantities gives a little flavour boost to stews. With dried tomatoes, the moisture is removed and the taste concentrated: they are simultaneously sweet and spicy, as well as delicious in salads, pasta dishes and tapenades.

recipes

Virgin tomato cocktail

For 2 cocktails

> 12 ripe tomatoes, cubed
> 1 clove of garlic, finely chopped
> 1 onion, chopped
> 1 tsp Tabasco
> salt and pepper to taste
> ice cubes (optional)

1   Mix the tomatoes, garlic, onion and Tabasco for about 1 minute in the blender.
2   Pour the cocktail through a sieve into highball glasses. Season with salt and pepper and serve with ice cubes.

Fresh sweet tomato milkshake

For 2 shakes

> 250ml (8.45 fl oz) milk
> 6 vine tomatoes, cubed
> 1 tbsp sugar
> juice of 1 lime
> salt and freshly ground pepper

1 Mix all the ingredients, except the salt and pepper, into a frothy mixture in the blender.
2 Pour through a sieve into two cups and season with salt and pepper.

Lukewarm oil-based tomato sauce

> 6 fragrant tomatoes
> 1 clove of garlic, finely chopped
> 2 tbsp corn oil
> 2 tbsp olive oil
> 1 tbsp white wine vinegar
> 1 tbsp Noilly Prat (or sherry)
> salt and freshly ground pepper
> 1 tbsp capers
> 1 tbsp finely chopped basil

1 Cut 2 tomatoes into quarters, remove the seeds and cores (retain) and cut the flesh into small cubes (the official term is brunoise). Cut the remaining tomatoes into pieces.
2 Cook the tomato pieces, including the seeds and juice from the brunoise, as well as the garlic into a thick purée on a low heat for a couple minutes.
3 Stir the purée through a sieve and spoon back into the pan. Add both the oils, wine vinegar and Noilly Prat (or sherry), and bring to the boil. Allow it to cook for 1 minute at a low heat while stirring continually.
4 Take the pan from the heat and stir in the capers, the tomato brunoise and basil, and season with salt and pepper. Serve lukewarm.

This dressing-like sauce tastes delicious with pasta or rice but is also delightful served with grilled meat or fish.

Gazpacho, cold Spanish tomato soup

> 1kg (2.2lb) fragrant tomatoes, cubed
> 2 cucumbers, peeled and seeded
> 1 red pepper, cubed
> 1 clove of garlic, peeled
> 250ml (10 fl oz) dry white wine
> several drops of Tabasco
> 1 tbsp rosé (or red wine vinegar)
> salt and pepper

1. For the garnish, chop a small bit of tomato, (unpeeled) cucumber and pepper into small cubes.
2. Crush the rest of the tomatoes, cucumber, pepper and garlic in the food processor.
3. Mash the mixture through a sieve and stir in the wine, Tabasco and rosé.
4. Season the gazpacho with salt and pepper, and leave it to chill completely in the fridge.
5. Garnish with vegetable cubes.

Just before serving, you could also add some crushed ice cubes to chill the gazpacho a little more.

Antiboise, tomato sauce from Antibes

> 3 pomodori tomatoes (plum tomatoes),
>   skinned, seeded and chopped into
>   small cubes
> 1 clove of garlic, chopped
> 10 basil leaves, finely chopped
> 3 tbsp olive oil
> balsamic vinegar and sea salt

1 Mix the tomato, garlic, basil and olive oil together, and season with sea salt and vinegar.

Antiboise is generally served as a garnish for fried or grilled fish such as sardines or sea bass, but it also tastes great with steak or lamb.

Spicy tomato salsa

> 100ml (3.38 fl oz) corn oil
> 6 fragrant tomatoes, chopped
> 1 onion, minced
> 3 red chilli peppers, cores removed
>   and chopped into strips
> 4 cloves of garlic, finely chopped
> 1 tsp sugar

1 Heat 1 tablespoon of oil in a pan and fry the tomato, onion, chilli pepper and garlic until the onion is transparent. Stir occasionally.
2 Purée the mixture with the rest of the oil and sugar into a smooth salsa in the blender.

Makes a great dip for tortilla chips.

Tomato Marmalade

> 1 kg (2.2 lb) tomatoes, peeled
> 750g (26oz) sugar
> peel and juice of 2 lemons

1 Mash the tomatoes with either a masher or a blender.
2 Mix the sugar together with the lemon peel and juice and stir into the tomato pulp. Cover and leave to stand for 12 hours.
3 Boil the mixture and leave to simmer on a low heat for one hour.
4 Pour the marmalade into well cleaned jars, close the lid immediately and leave to cool upside down. The marmalade can be kept unopened for about 1 month.

Tastes great with goat's cheese and toast.

Fresh tomato soup

> 1 tbsp olive oil
> 1 small onion, chopped
> 1 celery stalk,
>   chopped into small arches
> 1 clove of garlic, finely chopped
> 1kg (2.2lb) tomatoes, finely chopped
> 1litre (2 pints) chicken stock
> a small handful of basil, chopped
> 1 tbsp mozzarella, diced (optional)

1   Heat the olive oil in a large pan and fry the onion, celery and garlic until the onion is transparent. Stir in the tomato and sautée for another minute.
2   Add the chicken stock and simmer uncovered for 20 minutes on a moderate heat.
3   Purée the soup with a hand blender.
4   Heat the tomato soup through and garnish with basil and mozzarella.

Dried tomato pesto

> 4 tbsp chopped dried tomatoes
>   (see recipe on page 66)
> 50g (1.76 oz) Parmesan cheese
> 3 tbsp pine kernels,
>   roasted in an un-oiled pan
> 1 tbsp chopped basil
> ± 3 tbsp olive oil

1 Purée all the ingredients in a food processor into a smooth pesto.

Wonderful with pasta or on crostini.

Dried tomato salad dressing

> I egg yolk
> I tsp mustard
> I tsp honey
> 3 tbsp vegetable stock
> I tbsp white wine vinegar
> I tbsp chopped dried tomato
>   (see recipe on page 66)
> corn oil
> salt

1 With the hand blender, mix the egg yolk, mustard, honey, stock, vinegar and dried tomato.
2 Whilst the hand blender is on, slowly pour in as much oil as required until you have a lovely smooth dressing.
3 Taste and season with salt and add more oil or honey to taste.

Oven-roasted cherry tomatoes

> 1 punnet of cherry tomatoes (250g, 8.8 oz)
> 1 clove of garlic, chopped
> 1 tbsp sugar
> 4 tbsp olive oil
> sea salt
> a couple of rosemary sprigs,
> roughly chopped

1 Heat the oven to 200°C (400°F, gas mark 6).
2 Place the tomatoes in an oven dish and mix in garlic, sugar and olive oil.
3 Sprinkle with sea salt and place the rosemary on top. Roast the tomatoes for about 20 minutes in the oven.

Tomato carpaccio

> 3 beef tomatoes, in wafer-thin slices
> 1 tbsp black olives finelt chopped,
> 1 tsp capers
> 100g (3.5 oz) hard goat's cheese,
>   in cubes
> salt and pepper

1 Arrange tomato slices on 4 plates.
2 Sprinkle olives, capers, goat's cheese and some salt and ground pepper on top.

Stuffed tomatoes Caprese

> 4 beef tomatoes, tops removed
> and insides scooped out (keep the flesh)
> 1 ball of mozzarella, in small cubes
> a small handful of basil, chopped
> 2 tbsp olive oil
> Salt and pepper

1 Mix the tomato flesh with the mozzarella, basil and olive oil; season with salt and pepper.
2 Fill the tomatoes with this mixture.

`Caprese' (from `insalata Caprese', Capri-style salad) consists of tomato, mozzarella and basil: the Italian tricolour.

Tomato and roasted pepper salad with anchovy dressing

> 200ml (6.76 fl oz) olive oil
> 1 tbsp red wine vinegar
> 8 tinned anchovies, finely chopped
> 2 roasted red peppers*, cut into strips
> 4 tomatoes, cores removed
>   and in pieces
> 1 red onion, in thin rings
> 2 tbsp pitted black olives

1 Mix the oil, vinegar and anchovies to make a dressing.
2 Divide the pepper, tomato, onion and olives over 4 plates. Sprinkle the dressing on top.

Place the pepper(s) on a large piece of aluminium foil in a preheated oven at 200°C (400°F, gas mark 6). Roast for 30 minutes; fold the foil over to seal the peppers into a package. Leave the peppers to cool down in this way and then remove the skin, stalks and cores.

Tomato and cucumber salad with garlic and lemon dressing

> 6 vine tomatoes, sliced
> 1 cucumber, peeled and in thin slices
> 2 spring onions, in rings
> salt and freshly ground pepper

For the dressing:
> juice of 1 lemon
> 2 tbsp olive oil
> 1 clove of garlic, finely chopped
> 1 tsp honey

1 Mix the ingredients together well for the dressing.
2 Place the tomato slices and cucumber on 4 plates and sprinkle with dressing.
3 Scatter the spring onion on top; season with salt and pepper.

Sea bass and tomato casserole

> 4 sea bass filets of 150g (5.3 oz)
> 500g (1.1lb) tomatoes cut into quarters
> 1 red onion cut into half rings
> 3 tbsp olive oil
> ½ tbsp coarse mustard
> 2 tbsp dry white wine
> 1 clove of garlic, finely chopped
> 1 spring onion, in rings
> 1 tbsp lemon juice

1 Heat the oven to 180°C (350°F, gas mark 4).
2 Place the tomatoes, red onion and the sea bass in an oven dish.
3 Make a mixture of olive oil, mustard, wine and garlic, and pour over the fish and tomatoes. Cover the dish with aluminium foil.
4 Put the oven dish in the oven for about 15 minutes or until the fish is cooked.
5 Scatter the spring onion and just before serving sprinkle with lemon juice.

Serve with couscous or polenta and a fresh salad.

The most delicious ketchup ever

> ½ tsp mustard seed
> 5 dried pimentos
> 3 peppercorns
> 3 cloves
> I cinnamon stick
> I.5kg (3.3lbs) ripe tomatoes,
>   skinned and chopped coarsely
> I onion, minced
> 2 tsp salt
> I25 g (4.4I oz) sugar
> I50ml (5 fl oz) white wine vinegar

I   Place mustard seed, pimento, pepper, clove and cinnamon in the middle of a piece of cheesecloth and tie tightly with kitchen string.
2   Leave the tomatoes and onion to soften in a large pan at a moderate heat for 30 minutes.
3   Purée the tomato mixture with a hand blender and put back on the heat. Leave to reduce to a thick sauce. Stir regularly.
4   Stir the salt, sugar, vinegar and the spice ball into the tomato sauce and leave to simmer for an hour on a low heat.
5   Take the spice ball out of the pan, taste and if necessary season the ketchup with some more salt, vinegar or sugar.

Traditional tomato risotto
with mussels

> 2kg (4.4lbs) mussels
> 400ml (13 fl oz) dry white wine
> 1 onion, minced
> 1 carrot, finely chopped
> 1 leek, finely chopped
> A large bunch of parsley

For the tomato risotto
> 1 tbsp olive oil
> 2 tbsp butter

400g (14 oz) risotto rice <
(200ml (6.76 fl oz) stock from
the mussels)
1 small onion, chopped <
500ml (17 fl oz) fish stock <
500ml (17 fl oz) tomato juice <
4 tomatoes, core removed <
and in cubes
100g (3.5 oz) grated <
Parmesan cheese

1   Wash the mussels in cold running water and remove any broken or opened ones, which do not close again after a light tap on the work top surface.
2   Pour the wine for the mussels into a large pan, add the vegetables and the mussels and then bring to the boil. Cook for about 5 minutes until all the shells are open. Shake from time to time.
3   Strain the mussels but keep the stock. Measure out 200ml (6.76 fl oz) stock for the risotto. Take the mussels out of the shell (keep a couple for garnish).
4   For the risotto, heat the oil and a half a tablespoon of butter in a pan and add the rice. Stir continuously with a wooden spoon until the rice is very hot and the grains are transparent.
5   Mix the tomato juice into the fish stock.
6   Pour 200ml (6.76 fl oz) mussel stock into the rice and stir continuously until nearly all the liquid is absorbed. Add a good spoonful of tomato stock and continue to stir gently while the rice absorbs the stock. Keep adding the next spoonful of stock as soon as the previous is absorbed completely, until the rice is cooked but still has a little bit of a bite to it. This takes about 20 minutes. You may not need all the stock.
7   Mix the mussels, tomato and cheese into the risotto and leave everything to warm through.
8   Stir the rest of the butter into the risotto and then serve onto 4 plates. Garnish with the remaining mussels.

Tagliatelle with fresh tomato sauce

> 1 tbsp olive oil
> 1 large onion, finely chopped
> 1 clove of garlic, finely chopped
> 1 carrot, in small cubes
> 1 celery stalk, in small pieces
> a small handful of parsley, finely chopped
> 2 tbsp tomato purée
> 500g (1.1lb) ripe tomatoes,
>   cores removed and cut in cubes
> salt and pepper
> 400g (14 oz) tagliatelle
> 50g (1.76 oz) grated Parmesan cheese

1   Heat the oil in a pan and fry the onion and garlic until transparent. Add the carrot, celery and parsley and fry for 1 minute.
2   Stir the tomato purée and the tomato cubes into the vegetable mixture and fry for about 5 minutes on a medium heat stirring constantly. Season with salt and pepper; reduce the heat and leave to simmer for 30 minutes on a low heat. Stir from time to time.
3   Towards the end of the simmering time for the sauce, cook the tagliatelle al dente according to the instructions on the package.
4   Drain the pasta and mix in the sauce. Serve with parmesan cheese.

Fried tomato and aubergine salad

> 2 firm aubergines, in small cubes
> 1 tbsp olive oil
> 1 onion, chopped
> 2 cloves of garlic crushed
> 500g (1.1lb) tomatoes cut into pieces
> 2 tbsp chopped coriander
> Salt and pepper

1 Heat the oil and fry the aubergine for about 4 minutes until brown. Stir regularly.
2 Add the onion, garlic and tomato and fry until the onion is soft.
3 Stir in the coriander and season with salt and pepper. Put everything into a colander or sieve and leave to cool.

This salad is lovely with bread, but also tastes very good with pasta or rice.

Orange and tomato juice with basil

For 4 glasses

> a small handful of basil
> (keep some leaves for garnish)
> 500g (1.1lb) fragrant tomatoes
> cut into quarters
> 2 oranges, peeled and cut in quarters
> 2 tbsp chopped dried tomato
> (see recipe on page 66)

1 Juice all the ingredients in a juicer. Stir well and pour into 4 glasses. Garnish with basil.

Meatballs in tomato sauce

> 500g (1.1lb) minced (ground) veal
> 1 egg, gently beaten
> 100g (3.5 oz) breadcrumbs
> 2 tbsp parsley, chopped
> 2 cloves of garlic, chopped
> salt
> about 2 tbsp flour
> 1 tbsp olive oil

For the tomato sauce
> 1 carrot, in small pieces
> 1 onion, minced
> 500g (1.1lb) tomatoes,
>   chopped coarsely
> 100ml (3.38 fl oz) beef stock
> 2 tbsp tomato purée
> 100ml (3.38 fl oz) dry white wine

1 Mix the mince (ground veal) in with the egg, breadcrumbs, parsley, garlic and a little bit of salt. Shape into small balls and roll them in flour.
2 Heat the oil in a frying pan and fry the balls until brown, and then take them out of the pan.
3 For the sauce, heat the olive oil in the same pan and fry the carrot and onion until the onion is transparent. Add the tomatoes and fry for a couple of minutes.
4 Stir in the stock, tomato purée and white wine and simmer for about 10 minutes on low heat.
5 Spoon the meatballs carefully into the sauce and leave to simmer for another 10 minutes.

Tender chicken fillet with balsamic tomatoes

> 400g (14 oz) chicken fillets
> 100ml (3.38 fl oz) tomatoes
  coarsely chopped
> 2 tbsp capers
> 3 tbsp balsamic vinegar
> 1 tbsp olive oil
> 2 tbsp brown sugar
> salt and freshly ground pepper

1 Heat the oven to 200 °C (400°F, gas mark 6).
2 Cover the bottom of an oven dish with half of the tomatoes and place the chicken fillets on top.
3 Mix the rest of the tomato with the capers, balsamic vinegar, oil and sugar; then divide over the chicken fillets.
4 Bake in the oven for about 20 minutes until and then season with salt and freshly ground pepper.

Spanish tapas toast

For 12 portions

> ½ baguette, sliced
> olive oil
> 2 garlic cloves, peeled
> 2 ripe tomatoes, halved
> coarse sea salt

1 Heat the oven to 200 °C (400°F, gas mark 6).
2 Spread olive oil on the baguette and grill it in the oven on both sides until crisp.
3 Grate the garlic and the tomatoes over the baguette slices; making sure that the tomato is absorbed.
4 Sprinkle with a little bit of sea salt.

Snack salad with tomato and anchovy

For about 20 portions

> 16 tinned anchovies, coarsely chopped
> 12 black pitted olives
> and coarsely chopped
> 2 cloves of garlic, finely chopped
> 4 tomatoes, core removed
> and in cubes
> 1 tbsp capers
> 2 tbsp basil, chopped
> 1 baguette sliced

1 Mix all the ingredients together in a bowl.
2 Serve on a baguette.

Oven-dried pomodori tomatoes

> 100ml (3.38 fl oz) ripe pomodori tomatoes (plum tomatoes), halved lengthways
> coarse sea salt
> olive oil

1 Pre-warm the oven to 120°C (235°F, gas mark ½).
2 Place the tomatoes, cut side up, on a baking sheet.
3 Sprinkle them with sea salt and leave them to dry for 5-6 hours in the oven, with a tea-towel placed in the oven door.
4 Leave to cool down and sprinkle with a little bit of olive oil.

Corsican white broad-bean dish

> 400g (14 oz) dried white broad beans,
>   soaked overnight
> 2 tbsp olive oil
> 1 onion, chopped
> 2 garlic cloves, finely chopped
> 500g (1.1lb) tomatoes
>   cut into small pieces
> 1 spring onion cut in rings
> salt and pepper

1 Leave the broad beans to drain completely and then cook them in a pan of fresh water until just tender (about 1 to 1½ hours). Drain.
2 Heat the oil in a large pan and fry the onion and garlic until transparent. Stir in the tomatoes, broad beans and spring onion, and season with salt and pepper. Leave to simmer for 20 minutes on a low heat.

Also tastes delicious as a cold salad.

Summer potato casserole with pak choi and tomato

> 1kg (2.2lbs) potatoes, peeled and in small cubes
> 100ml (3.38 fl oz) milk
> 1 tbsp olive oil
> ½ tbsp mustard
> salt and pepper
> 1 large or 2 small pak choi, cut into fine strips
> 4 tomatoes cut into pieces

1 Cook the potatoes, drain and mash into a purée with milk, oil and mustard. Season with salt and pepper.
2 Stir the pak choi and tomato into the purée, warm quickly and serve immediately.

Hearty tomato soup with meatballs

> 1 tbsp olive oil
> 1 onion, minced
> 2 garlic cloves, finely chopped
> 500g (1.1lb) tomatoes, in small pieces
> 1 leek, finely chopped
> 2 sticks of celery, sliced
> 500ml (1 pint) vegetable stock
> 200g (7oz) minced meat (ground beef)
> salt and pepper

1   Heat the oil in a large pan and fry the onion and garlic until transparent. Add the tomatoes, leek and celery and leave to fry for 5 minutes. Douse with the stock, boil and then lower the heat.
2   Season the mince (ground beef) with salt and pepper, and roll into little balls.
3   Stir the meatballs through the soup and cook for 5 minutes on a low heat.

Herb butter with dried tomato

> 150 g (5.3oz) soft butter
> 1 clove of garlic, crushed
> 2 tbsp dried tomato, chopped
  (see recipe on page 66)
> 2 tbsp basil, finely chopped
> salt

1   Mix together the butter, garlic, dried tomato and basil in the blender or with a hand food processor. Season with salt.
2   Serve the butter in a small dish.

Nice on a warm baguette.

Quick Italian vegetable dish

> 1 tbsp olive oil
> 1 courgette, in thin slices
> 4 tomatoes, in thin slices
> 1 clove of garlic, minced
> 1 onion, minced
> 100g (3.5 oz) fontina
> (Italian melting cheese) cut into slices
> basil, cut into strips

1 Heat the oven to 200 °C (400°F, gas mark 6).
2 Heat the oil in a frying pan and fry the onion and garlic until transparent. Mix in the courgette and fry for 1 minute.
3 Transfer the courgette mixture into an oven dish and place the tomato slices on top.
4 Cover with fontina and put in the oven for 2 minutes. Sprinkle with basil.

Oven-baked stuffed tomatoes with spinach and egg

> 4 beef tomatoes, tops removed and insides scooped out (keep the flesh)
> salt and pepper
> 1 tbsp olive oil
> 1 clove of garlic, finely chopped
> 1 anchovy fillet (from a tin)
> 100g (3.5 oz) spinach, chopped
> 4 eggs

1 Heat the oven to 180°C (350°f, gas mark 4).
2 Sprinkle the insides of the tomatoes with salt and pepper.
3 Heat the oil in a pan and fry the garlic and anchovy until the anchovy dissolves.
4 Stir in the spinach and allow to wither. Drain in a colander.
5 Mix the tomato flesh into the spinach and then fill the tomatoes up halfway with this mixture. Put in an oven dish.
6 On each tomato, break open an egg and then put the dish in the oven until the eggs are firm (about 10 minutes).

Tomato tarte tatin

> 1 tbsp olive oil
> 2 tbsp dried tomato pesto (see page 32)
> 500g (1.1lb) cherry tomatoes (2 punnets)
> leaves from a couple of sprigs of thyme
> (keep some of the leaves for garnish)
> salt and pepper
> 6 sheets of puff pastry, rolled out
> to a piece slightly larger than the pie dish

> *pie dish of 26 cm (10 in.) in diameter,*
> *greased with olive oil*

1 Heat the oven to 200 °C (400°F, gas mark 6).
2 Sprinkle some thyme on the bottom of the pie dish and place the tomatoes closely together. Spread with pesto.
3 Place the piece of pastry on top of the tomatoes. Push the overhanging pastry against the inside edge of the pie dish and bake the pie for 10 minutes in the oven. Reduce the oven temperature to 160°C (315°F, gas mark 2½) and bake the pie for another 30 minutes once until golden brown and done.
4 Turn the tarte tatin over onto a dish and garnish with thyme.

Quick hearty soup with broad beans

> I tbsp olive oil
> I clove of garlic, finely chopped
> I onion, chopped
> 500g (1.1lb) tomatoes, in pieces
> I litre (2 pints) vegetable stock
> I tin white broad beans (400 g, 14 oz),
> drained
> a small handful of celery leaves,
> chopped

1 Heat the oil in a large pan; and then fry the garlic, onion and tomatoes until the onion is transparent (about 5 minutes).
2 Pour in the stock and simmer for 5 more minutes.
3 Purée the soup with a hand blender and if desired pour through a sieve.
4 Add the broad beans and celery and heat the soup thoroughly.

Sweet and sour tomato caponata

> I tbsp olive oil
> I red onion, chopped into half rings
> 4 cloves of garlic, I finely chopped
>   and 3 peeled
> I yellow pepper, cores removed,
>   cut into strips
> I green pepper, cores removed,
>   cut into strips
> 500g (1.1lb) vine tomatoes, in quarters
> a small handful of black olives
> a small handful of green olives
> I tbsp white wine vinegar
> I tsp sugar

1 Heat the oil in a pan and fry the onion and all the garlic quickly. Stir in the pepper strips and
   tomatoes carefully and fry everything together quickly (about I minute). The vegetables
   must remain extremely crisp.
2 Remove the pan from the heat, mix in the olives and then spoon everything into a dish.
3 Beat the wine vinegar and sugar together and then pour over the vegetables. Leave covered
   to marinate for a couple of hours, preferably overnight.

Tastes delicious as a side dish or antipasti both warm and cold.

Chinese tomato soup with chicken and rice noodles

> 1 tbsp olive oil
> 1 onion, minced
> 1 clove of garlic, finely chopped
> 500g (1.1lb) tomatoes, chopped in small pieces
> 500ml (1 pint) tomato juice
> 500ml (1 pint) chicken stock
> 3 tbsp brown sugar
> 2 tbsp ketchup
> 2 tbsp (rice) vinegar
> 1 tsp sambal
> 300g (10.5oz) cooked chicken (thigh), in cubes
> 1 leek, very finely chopped
> 100g (3.5 oz) rice noodles

1   Heat the oil in a large pan and fry the onion, garlic and tomato until the onion is transparent (about 5 minutes).
2   Pour in the tomato juice and stock, and leave for 5 minutes.
3   Purée the soup with a hand blender and if required pour through a sieve.
4   Heat the soup once more and stir in the brown sugar, ketchup, vinegar and sambal. Bring to the boil and stir until the sugar has dissolved.
5   Mix the chicken, leek and rice noodle into the soup and cook until the noodles are completely done (see package for the exact cooking time).

Tomato chutney

> 1 tbsp olive oil
> 1kg (2.2lb) tomatoes, in small pieces
> 2 cloves of garlic, finely chopped
> 1 onion, chopped
> 250g (8.8oz) brown sugar
> 1cm (0.4 inch) ginger root, grated
> 2 tbsp black olives, chopped
> pinch of salt
> 100ml (3.38 fl oz) white wine vinegar

1 Heat the oil in a large pan and add the tomatoes stirring constantly. Then stir in the garlic and onion and fry for 1 minute.
2 Stir the sugar, ginger, olives, salt and vinegar into the tomato mixture. Simmer for about 30 minutes on a low heat until the chutney thickens.
3 Pour the chutney into very clean jars. Shut the lids tight immediately and leave to cool upside down.

Tomato soup with oven-roasted tomatoes

> 1kg (2.2lb) fragrant tomatoes, halved
> 1 ½ tbsp oregano, finely chopped
> 1 ½ tbsp basil, finely chopped
> 2 cloves of garlic, finely chopped
> 1 tsp sugar
> 1 tbsp olive oil
> 1 litre (2 pints) vegetable stock
> yoghurt or cream (optional)

1 Heat the oven to 120°C (230°F, gas mark ¼).
2 Place the tomatoes, cut side up, on a baking sheet. Sprinkle with the herbs, garlic and sugar, and then roast for about 45 minutes in the oven.
3 Bring the stock to the boil and stir in the tomatoes, along with their cooking juices. Cook on a low heat for 30 minutes.
4 Purée the soup with a hand blender and if desired pour through a sieve. Serve with a dollop of either yoghurt or cream to taste.

Oven-roasted tomato sorbet

> 1 ½kg (3.3lbs) ripe tomatoes,
> halved and cores removed
> 1 tbsp balsamic vinegar
> 125 ml (4.2 fl oz) water
> 1 tbsp lemon juice
> a couple of drops of
> Worcestershire sauce
> Salt and ground pepper

1 Heat the oven to 200 °C (400°F, gas mark 6).
2 Place the tomatoes, cut side up, on a baking sheet and drizzle the balsamic vinegar on top.
   Roast them in the oven for 10 minutes.
3 Remove the skin of the tomatoes and purée them in the blender or with a hand blender
   along with the water, lemon juice and Worcestershire sauce. Season with salt and
   ground pepper.
4 Leave the mixture to cool down completely and spoon into a deep-freeze container. Leave
   for about 3 hours. Stir every hour with a fork.

Nice with fish or seafood.

Rice salad

> 200g (7oz) long grain rice
> 1 spring onion, sliced into thin rings
> 1 green pepper, core removed
  and cut into strips
> 1 yellow pepper, core removed
  and cut into strips
> 3 tomatoes, cores removed
  and cut into pieces
> 1 tbsp coriander, finely chopped

For the dressing
> 3 tbsp corn oil
> 1 tbsp rice vinegar
> 1 tsp mustard
> salt and freshly ground black pepper

1   Cook the rice for 10-12 minutes until almost cooked. The grains must still have a little bite.
    Wash the rice under cold water and leave to drain completely.
2   Mix the rice, spring onion, pepper, tomato and coriander in a large bowl.
3   Make a dressing by shaking all the ingredients together in a closed jar. Stir into the rice.
4   Cover and leave for at least one hour in the fridge.